Malala's Magic Pencil

MALALA YOUSAFZAI

Illustrated by KERASCOËT

PUFFIN

Do you believe in magic?

When I was younger, I used to watch a TV show about a boy who had a magic pencil. If he was hungry, he drew a bowl of curry, and it appeared. If he and his friends were in danger, he drew a police officer. The boy was a little hero, always protecting people who needed help.

How I wanted a magic pencil, too!

If I had a magic pencil, I would use it to . . .

. . . put a lock on my door, so my brothers couldn't bother me.

. . . stop time, so I could sleep an extra hour every morning.

... erase the smell of the
rubbish dump near our house.

And I would use it to make other people happy.

I would draw . . .

. . . the most beautiful dresses
in the world for my mother.

. . . the best buildings in the valley for my father, so he could
open many schools where children would study for free.

. . . a proper ball, so my brothers and I no longer had
to play with an old sock stuffed with rubbish.

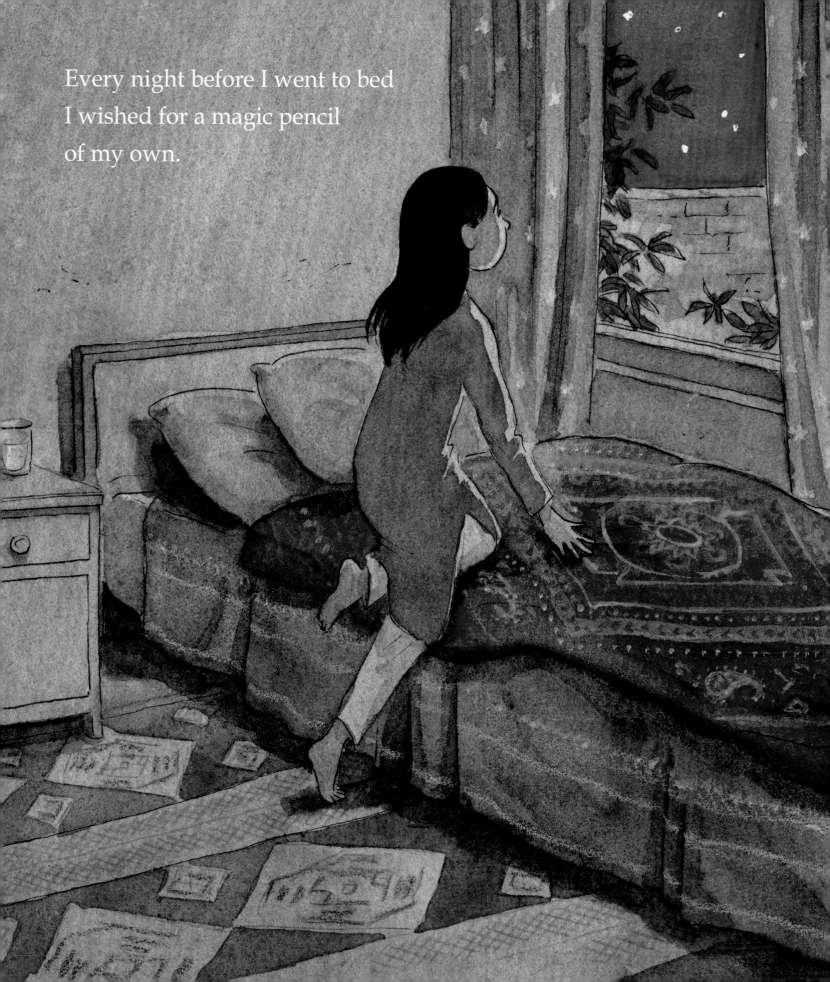

Every night before I went to bed
I wished for a magic pencil
of my own.

And every morning I would wake up
and check my cupboard.

But the magic pencil was never there.

One day, I was throwing away potato peelings and eggshells at the dump. I was wrinkling my nose, swatting away flies, and making sure I didn't step on anything dirty in my nice shoes, when I saw a girl about my age sorting rubbish into piles.

Nearby, boys were fishing for metal scraps using magnets on strings.

When my father returned home from work, I told him what I'd seen. It made him sad.

"*Aba*?" I said.

"Yes, *jani*?" he said back. I always liked when he called me "dear one".

"Why haven't I seen that girl in my class?"

"Because . . ." he said, but he didn't finish right away. "Because, *jani*, in our country not everyone sends their daughters to school. And some children must work to support their family. Those boys will sell the metal scraps they find. If they went to school, their families would go hungry."

School was my favourite place. But I had never considered myself lucky to be able to go.

My father had always said, "Malala will live free as a bird."

Now I wondered how free I'd truly be.

That night I thought about families who didn't have enough food. And the girl who couldn't go to school. And even about how when I was older I would be expected to cook and clean for my brothers, because where I came from many girls weren't allowed to become what they dreamed of.

I knew then that if I had the magic pencil I would use it to draw a better world, a peaceful world.

First, I would erase war, poverty and hunger. Then I would draw girls and boys together as equals.

Over the next few years, instead of wishing
for a magic pencil every night, I worked hard
in school every day. I wanted to be one of the
top students in my class.

But soon powerful and dangerous men declared that girls
were forbidden from attending school.

They walked the streets of our city
now. They carried weapons.

One by one, girls stopped coming to school.

"*Aba*, where are all the students?"

"They don't feel safe here any more, *jani*."

How could a few men stop all the girls in our valley from going to school? If more people knew what was happening to us, I thought, they might help.

Wishing wasn't enough. Someone needed to speak out.

Why not me?

I wrote about what it felt like to be scared to walk to school and how some of my friends had moved away because of the threat they faced in our city. I wrote about how much I loved school and how proud I was of my uniform.

Once I started writing, I didn't stop. I wrote speeches and travelled around my country, sharing my story – I even talked to a reporter from a famous international newspaper. People actually wanted to learn about my life! I spoke for all the girls in my valley who couldn't speak for themselves.

My voice became so powerful that dangerous men
tried to silence me.

But they failed.

And now my voice is louder than ever. Louder because people have joined me, and together we make a chorus, standing up for what we believe. We . . .

    . . . raise our voices for those in need.

        . . . help people in danger, even if they are an ocean away.

           . . . think of the world as a family.

Do you still believe in magic?

I do.

I wrote alone in my room, but people all over the world were reading my story. Millions now know it and help me spread my message of hope.

I had at last found the magic I was looking for – in my words and in my work.

I am Malala. I've always wished I could make the world a more peaceful place . . .

. . . and every day I work to make my wish come true.

One child, one teacher,
one book and one pen
can change the world.

Dear friend,

As a child, I used to watch a TV show called *Shaka Laka Boom Boom*. It was about a boy named Sanju, who could make anything real by drawing it with a magic pencil he found. Sanju and his friends were always getting into trouble, and the magic pencil would help them get out of it, but my early childhood was mostly trouble-free.

I grew up in the beautiful Swat Valley in northwest Pakistan, the sister of two cheeky little brothers and the only daughter of a resilient mother and inspiring father who was a school headteacher.

Trouble came to my valley when I was ten years old, and girls were forbidden from going to school. At first I thought, *What can I do? I'm just a child*. As I watched my father speak out for girls' education, I realized I had a voice, too, and I wanted to use it. I believed then, as I believe now, that all children should have access to education.

When we are young, we feel powerless. We rely on adults to do the serious work. However, when real danger threatened my right to go to school, I felt stronger than ever, and I found power in my voice. Once, I wished for Sanju's magic pencil. Now I know that when you find your voice, every pencil can be magic.

I hope that my story inspires you to find the magic in your own life and to always speak up for what you believe in. Magic is everywhere in the world – in knowledge, beauty, love, peace. The magic is in you, in your words, in your voice.

Malala

ABOUT MALALA YOUSAFZAI

Malala Yousafzai first came to public attention by writing for BBC Urdu about life under the Taliban using the pen name Gul Makai. The Taliban had forbidden girls in her region from going to school. Soon, she began to speak publicly about girls' education in her community. In October 2012, Malala was targeted by the Taliban and attacked as she was returning home from school. She miraculously survived.

Malala and her family now live in Birmingham, England, and she travels the world speaking about the importance of education for all. In 2013, she started Malala Fund, which has since opened schools for girls in Pakistan, as well as in Lebanon and Jordan for Syrian refugees. Of the over 130 million girls who are out of school, many are refugees.

In recognition of her courage and advocacy, Malala was honoured with the National Youth Peace Prize in Pakistan in 2011 and won both the International Children's Peace Prize and the Amnesty International Ambassador of Conscience Award in 2013. In 2014, she became the youngest-ever recipient of the Nobel Peace Prize (shared with Indian children's activist Kailash Satyarthi). In 2017, Malala became the youngest-ever UN Messenger of Peace, with a special focus on girls' education.

As a young child

With my school trophies

With my family in Birmingham, England

This book was edited by Farrin Jacobs and designed by Sasha Illingworth. The production was supervised by Erika Schwartz, and the production editor was Jen Graham. The illustrations for this book were done in ink and watercolour on cold-pressed paper by Kerascoët and separated by Naëwë. The text was set in Book Antiqua, and the display type was hand-lettered by Sarah J. Coleman. Family photo by Mark Tucker; all other photos courtesy of the author.

Penguin
Random House
UK

PUFFIN BOOKS • UK | USA | Canada | Ireland | Australia | India | New Zealand | South Africa • Puffin Books is part of the Penguin Random House group of companies whose addresses can be found at global.penguinrandomhouse.com • First published in the USA by Little, Brown and Company, a division of Hachette Book Group, Inc., and in Great Britain by Puffin Books 2017 • This edition published 2019 • Text and illustrations copyright © Salarzai Limited, 2017 • Cover and interior illustrations by Kerascoët • Cover art © Salarzai Limited, 2017 • Cover design by Sasha Illingworth • Cover copyright © Hachette Book Group, Inc., 2017 • All rights reserved • The moral right of the author and illustrator has been asserted • A CIP catalogue record for this book is available from the British Library • ISBN: 978-0-241-32257-4 • All correspondence to: Puffin Books, Penguin Random House Children's, 80 Strand, London WC2R 0RL • Printed in China • 001